War Dreams

War Dreams

ISBN: 978-1-7330703-0-0

War Dreams

by Samantha Geovjian Clarke

Dedication

For Joel, who knows why

For Kay's Bar, an unexpected commons

For John, Yasmeen, Josh, James, Becca, Doug, Tonya, Yasmeen, my Nana, and my mother, the beautiful swan Daleen Elizabeth

For *Build,* which published some of these poems in their Poetry and Ecosocialism editions and whose members, I believe, are actively trying to build the *we* that we need

For Andrew Hozier-Byrne, Irène Mathieu, Adam Tod Brown, Natalie Wynn and Olly Thorn

For everyone who supports me online and beyond

Samantha Geovjian Clarke

Survivor's Guilt

I feel a Coming--
not first, or Second,
not the seventh mass one
or the false return of *making it so again*
but dreams of war,
a repetition too deep a brown
to believe how many times,
how many witches,
have felt its approach before.
And yet, again?
And perhaps, more?

**

My ancestors don't know what to say to me.
They pull hard into now,
every part aching like old voices,
just to tell me they're sorry.
Sorry for what?
Sorry I will know what they knew,
sorry I will smell flesh and soil and fire,
sorry I have no cross to wear
around my neck.
Sorry for coming before.
Survivors' guilt from the victims of genocide.

**

It will be barren.
Ash will float, suspended
like our screams
in dark air.
Some of the people who deserve to
will be in desperate, anguished guilt
and more of us
will ask false gods what have we done
when we have done nothing at all,
at most.

**

Those of us who can remember the smell
of honeysuckle,
the juice of overripe peaches
and blueberries,
meadows full of tall wildflowers,
mountain laurel, cherry trees,
jambalaya, ice cream, mujadarrah,
listening to Miles Davis on a summer afternoon,
will reach through time and ache
just to say we're sorry.

Andromeda

We do not dance the way planets do,
anymore. Once,
through most of our moment in universal history,
we looked up, and around,
instead of inward.
Individualism, they insist, is the pinnacle
of human liberty,
but I've heard the voice of a man
who lived in a box alone, for decades.
It was as far from the voice of planets
and stars
as the cold steel spires on the tops of skyscrapers,
screeching in the high wind.
No one is free alone.
Especially not bodies made of skin and
water and iron-rich organs,
souls made of magnolias and pears,
spirits made of blue and the twinkle of a creek
in the moonlight.
We do not dance the way planets do
because we have forgotten what it means to
be a galaxy.

XXXI

Here is my shame:
love is the one thing I have failed to constrict

I love you the way of some future, or past
that uses more than one word to
describe that tightening tether between breasts,
hearts pulling from behind.

I love you like the copper soothing strains
of a faint violin,
like the flaking of shortbread,
like the steady paleness of a candle
in a low-lit room.

I love you like the gentle yellow of safety,
like the embrace of *I miss you.*

I even love you like a hand a moment too long on my back,
like eyes meeting in a knowing instant.

Ain't no sunshine when she's gone
whispers through me when my mind wanders
and the weight of his heart - *would he
understand?* - follows after.

My shame. My burden. A beautiful bond,
watered down, filtered through today.

**

Once, you and he made the room yellow, in
hushed tones, sentries at self-selected posts
sheltering me momentarily from the stray bullets
and shells I sometimes fail to dodge on my own.

He: winter, blue, brazen and forceful

You: broiling, tender, the slow moments of summer

How can I understand the ways I need you both?

Some things are wrong only because
they're out of time.

Arhythmic

touch of fall, like fresh bread
warm by its chill

why can I smell aging
in June,
when life should be going to prom,
not retiring?

In February, I felt the untimely summer glory
of the sun hot upon me

the world seems to spin irregular these days,
death and rebirth erratic,
the way stress makes menstruation arhythmic

I can feel an ending
and every witch I know feels it too

every fruit that falls carries a seed
that may never find root

may our seed know a beginning

For Aaliyah, for the future

Whether nature or nurture I may never know,
but heavy in the uterus I carry--me, or mine?--
is the sadness of a womb that will never hold,
breasts that will never be pulled,
hips that will never be settled by small thighs,
encircling

There is a universe where we married, settled in the valley
near your sister and our niece,
had a child of our own
and named her Aaliyah Nadezhda Geovjian Monroe

There is another universe where marriage doesn't matter
and having a child is beautiful, human,
something you can do in the city
and keep writing your poetry

but we live in a universe where the most human choice
is to deny our bodies their pleasure,
to use them instead for war
and, if we're lucky, for the relief
of a little bit of pain

We must find other meanings for love-making,
enter one another with veils on
and pretend our organs don't have voices

I fight for a simple aim:
may the future never deny the world a child
for fear of her fate in it

With the Sun

Give me life
before the sun rises

learn me, teach me
your ins and outs,
ridges,
the way lamplight bounces brighter
from your light skin
than from mine

The world burns outside;
the sun beats hotter than ever before
and movement is beginning--
perhaps not fast enough

but we both know who will be there

See me now, feel me, enter and cry out--
joy and grief entwined in one brief, tangible instant
as we realize what is not; what could be
what we will never know

with the sun, we will fight
for what we will never have

XXXII*

Survival translates across worlds, across time.
Make beauty necessary; make necessity beautiful
she whispered to me from across the continent,
telling stories of stones
and the way young shoots push their way into the sun
  between them.

Her weight is the same as mine; the same as my father's.

I can tell who will understand me
by the way they look at sunshine
and by what they think of when they cry

and I can see the gloppy varnish
dripping down the sides of buildings, people, objects
that were brought into the world to mimic beauty, or
  necessity.

A barn outside of Williamsburg, whitewashed, the roof
  sinking in the middle
and the grass overgrown around the edges.
Steve's old pickup, the back rusting and the paint chipped.
A mobile home, tired and faded, at the edge
of the Flathead Valley,
its closest neighbors the rocky mountains of Montana.

The way your grey hairs are growing in silver
and your hands find mine in the dark.

Fill me with the joy of survival;
let me sing to the tattered glory of simply
continuing to be.

For Anne Michaels

Perverted

I blushed, and buried my face in your chest
in the stolen hours of the morning
when only lovers and bartenders are still awake

I know, I'm disgusting
I said for the last ten years of my life,
and again to you

I am sorry the perversion of this world
has perverted me too

It's okay if you pretend you don't like it

Clean Water

Concrete lies upon the earth heavy,
not with the weight of a baby on her mama's chest
but awkward, burdensome, flattening
like a pack too big for a mule
or an encyclopedia pressed upon a clover

who could not feel this weight upon their organs
looking out over a vast plain of smooth grey?

who could step onto earth
and not feel a shout of joy spring up
from every joint in their body?

For being so alone, we are awfully crowded

At least let us have poetry
and clean water

Seam

Shades of green at different heights, and
bits of sidewalk in different shades,
remade over time,
tell stories so many people overlook.

Looking at cracks in the pavement,
discolored bits, a broken pattern,
I feel a profound love.
This--the scar tissue of survival--
is the beauty of built-upon,
the non-mathematical seam
of healing.

It's as impossible to ignore as
the crinkles around your eyes.

**

Patchwork lover, rebuilt friend.
Reworked over years, pulled apart, grown fresh
here or there;
a limb or an organ at a time.

Bless those eyes, which have seen themselves
in different forms.
Bless that heart, which has broken
again and again.
Bless that mind, which looks for answers
in all the crevices.

Haywire Minds

Red wine in coffee mugs,
makeshift tea-and-whiskey cocktails a little too early for
  summer,
the nicest IPA the bodega carried
at the kitchen table,
or in sweaters on your porch

booze with flavor but mostly with purpose
applied with understanding
to the weights we both carry

you told me once how you control your haywire mind
by sending it out of control, with lines or with vapor,
by powder or pill

I wanted to tell you how I do it too,
with my body, with pain, with submission
but how could I pull myself apart like that
without driving you away, or worse,
misleading you?

I long to open my soul
in a way you would be willing to see

how can I undress before you in earnest
without making you shade your eyes?

We hesitate superficially, treading too carefully
around the specter of bodies,
warning ourselves away from intimacy
and conflating opening

with lips

you are a song I can't quite remember

only refrain from eluding me, my gaze,
let me show myself, be
and rest that haywire mind by mine

Bush Did 9/11

The dystopian *they* of dark hallways,
shadowed mercenaries, cold suits
and earpieces
follows, nagging, despite the high gaslighting
of a world that screams conspiracy!
at anyone who is afraid--
what is the difference between lizard people
and the CIA?

Someday, I may disappear,
and to know that is to fight with integrity.

We make inventions when we see only visions,
the art of the psychic paranoid,
the way there is sometimes more truth in a metaphor
than a newspaper headline.

What is true, and what is truer?

There are prisons, and graveyards, full of people
who would at least agree on one thing:
it's not for no reason.

Start Wearing Purple

I found a long piece of shimmery purple fabric
and I wrapped it around my shoulders.

I declared my right to finery, to femininity;
drizzled myself with shine
and walked with straight shoulders

I heard you, Eugene--
I've started wearing purple--
for you,
for my ancestors and for yours

I don't think you knew
you were telling me *you deserve the color of royalty*

but I stood before you, soaked in wine,
breathless,
knew your people and mine
were more similar than different
and heard *our olive skin deserves purple*

and I thought of you as I donned a queen's scarf
over my peasant clothes

for Gogol Bordello*

The Weight of Daytime*

Longing for nighttime spears of beauty,
moonlight slipping into unexpected places,
rustles and cracks seldom heard
when diurnal creatures are awake
and movement pounds, stampedes and cascades--
here, now, it slithers; stirs; tiptoes
through lacy shadows.

I long for night the way I long for words;
the chosen rarely enough--
is it language leaping for a nick in a rock face,
grasping for, fumbling, falling short?
Or is it the way my foot taps
on the bar stool while my pen flies,
recklessly, lunging too far, too fast?

**

La hija de la diaspora
words I only know how to say in the languages
of the continent we escaped to,
words foreign even to the indigenous of this place.
Words sung with pride by women
who know where they are from.

My mouth has formed around words
it was never meant for,
my eyebrows hold expressions my nana
would never have understood.

My face, so much clay, was molded
by fingers both hostile and foreign,
both bitter and lost,
and it has only been sadness and pomegranates
that have spoken to me in a language
I can understand.

I was born seeing, but I have become blind.
Like my nana, I lean too heavily
upon my third eye;
the way the weight of unspoken tongues
shows me, pulls, the truth that others don't,
or don't know how to, tell.

**

The eerie coherency of advertisements,
how some 20 year-old intern tells clever jokes
on a major corporation's Twitter account,
how the posters in the mall pluck at my eyes
despite my pressing shame.

What kind of poet would not crawl
in the bones--most of her bones--
that know what it is to pierce with words;
the sap-heavy weight of guilt and repulsion
at the closeness of such corruption?

These words follow me, chasing out the words
of the forest, of nighttime, of lakes
and of breezes in a wetlands.
In the cluttered din of words,
cheap knick-knacks gathering dust on shelves,

how can I find my foothold;
my gem;
my Baron and Louise
in love in an antique shop?

These days,
glasses don't foam,
berries don't burst with sweetness,
rivers don't lap at shorelines.
He doesn't love me
the way I thought he would.
Words are rarely enough
and night feels as distant
as the way I used to write poems.

Curlers and Henna

And why shouldn't I?
What does this body have, or hold,
that it doesn't deserve?

What does *acting as if* do
that just *acting* doesn't do better?

Check it: punk meets vintage;
feminine forest hoodlum;
thick-ass hair curled up
into a big, tangly, glorious mess:
black roots showing true colors shamelessly
under henna-red ends.

I can fake my way to genuine.

I can call up legends I only know in my limbs,
paint them onto my eyelids
and wrap them around my hips.

Who cares if they're validated
when I know they're shared by every ghost
that whispers in my ear?

How Acid Taught Me the Severity of My Daddy Issues

After
I was born again--
not like Kirk but like
the caterpillar,
an overused metaphor
precisely because everyone knows
what it means to loop through time
in waves of color
in tears numb, waterfalls down a face
you forget exists,
forget what it looks like,
and to grow new limbs
that don't move how you want
or expect--
after that, I looked up with wide eyes
and I saw you.
I knew who you were.
You weren't there the first time I was born,
but this time Gaia and Uranus both
looked kindly upon me.
Womb, trauma, entering, safety. Recovery.
A process disrupted during my mother's
childbirth, but remade in one night
when we swallowed the way the world breathes.

War Dreams

They felt it, in the 60s, the mushrooms
both of freedom and destruction

individual release, collective end
collective sensation, individual terror

is it even so simple now, our war dreams?
My brother pulses with endings too, in his share of the sight
our nana passed on to us both,
but he sees a far different enemy than I do

it's hard to tell anymore what we share,
even our brown skin spelling different words
upon his head than upon mine
but blood boils, thick and hot,
and I know he remembers better than he foresees

**

I was telling you how, like the Gestapo,
border control agents were assuring parents
that they were just taking the children to bathe
before sending them to separate prisons--
mothers and fathers only hours later realizing
they weren't coming back

I confessed my instinct--
or perhaps paranoia--to flee

there is a voice inside me, only part
my own, that says firmly
not to me

Argue all day the theory of fascism, argue
what it is, or isn't,
but children are in cages,
great black eyes like my own, like my brother's,
like the children my great-grandmother knew who didn't
  make it out

they told the Jews who fled, before the camps,
that they were paranoid too

and I have seen enough to know
how quietly I could disappear

XXXIII

There is a bit of me--
not fingertips or toes,
or the closed places within me,
but a bit of my soul--
that looks for you.
Looks for you within you.
Looks into your eyes,
looks later into memories of you,
digs through rubble and clutter
to find your seed; your sapphire;
your inner call.
How, and where, and why, are you?
And why do I need you?
I was never prepared to blush for you.

Make of me my undoing,
pull and tear into my *why*
to take of me what I long to give you.

An open heart. A self-sabotage risk.
An experiment with what love means
when we take it out of the dictionary.

**

I want to open my eyes wide to you.
I want to feel your hand
on the back of my neck.
I want to nod and tell you, *yes.*

Bodies: always getting in the way.

Hold me from across the room.
Love me touchless.
Make our everything intangible.
I never expected to feel you
in my shoulders; in the heat of my heart.

Will I ever know
who is worth the risk of contact?

No to Thrones and Dominions, to Principalities and Powers

Day by day, and with each passing moment,
comfort and trembling intertwine
in dustbin memories
and the way the mind holds habits like a muscle.

The solution to my trials
was also the source of them;
the end no kind of beginning
to start from,
the crowns and the thrones
holding no pull that a world without concrete
could not surpass.

I ran to, and from, at once.
I tried to untangle my mind by armoring it,
by framing it,
and finally, by begging for peace.
I found only a hiding place.

The legend: the first follower saw the corruption,
led a charge to overthrow
the high king,
and was thrown into eternal prison.
The devil: a freedom fighter.

Changing Winds

Leaves pull one another along into the drawing
fingers of the wind.
The ligament I tore years ago, slipping
off a rock on my way down a mountain
and climbing back up it on that ripped knee,
groans gently at me.
The pressure has fallen; the urgency has risen.

**

I can feel it, the camps, and the cages;
the horrors obscured through branches,
visible only in glimpses--
a man stolen to be deported while bringing his laboring
  wife
to the hospital,
a little girl told not to speak to the press
on threat of never seeing her mama again.
Gray upon my mind, dark and wet,
the way black locust trees sink into the wetlands.

I use my injuries as a weather-vane:
blood and bone groaning at vibrations
in the atmosphere; the cells I started with
and the cells I grew
remembering what's to come.

Too Many Stones

Kay's Bar--since 1934
remarkable only because it is anathema,
this small wooden hole
with bright green, plastic awnings
and cheap vinyl barstools
has become the last remaining place
where everybody knows your name
and where I don't see the difference
between myself, the plumber, the software developer
and the bartender

who knew you could tell a story about the commons
until there were enclosures?

I'll let you buy me a drink here

you'll let me read, until your friends convince you
to come talk to me

let's talk politics
while the Alabama Shakes play over the speakers
and the bartender eyes us
and turns down the lights

**

We locked eyes across the worn carpet seats of the bus,
at night,

when the old man at the back tried to help you with
  directions--
you, with your long, curly hair, full breasts, and a bright pink
  bracelet--
and called you sir.

Your eyes, in that moment, were the torn of
he's trying to help
and, but, your dignity

You, with the patience of a goatherd,
corrected him only once
and then accepted that he hadn't heard
and still let him help you find your way.

After you left, he was still wondering aloud about your
  route,
sprinkling his concerned words with little,
accidental poison darts of hes and hims.

I remembered your grace, and tried to both channel and
  defend it
when I turned to him and said--
thank you so much for helping her find her way

Oh, I suppose she was a she,
he said, a bit startled

--one kind old man at a time

**

You couldn't help yourself--you giggled at the sight
of me, naked, reading *The Myths of Male Dominance* in
 bed
while still wearing the collar you put me in, hours before,
when you called me your pet and pushed into my knowing.

This perfectly compatible contradiction
makes up my being--
why shouldn't I search for the answer to my subjugation
in both theory books
and the pressing of your fingers into my flesh?

Nothing defeats those who would crush you
like making a game of the crushing.

The slave earns freedom, of the will at least,
by taking and making of slavery
a choice

I choose subjugation at this moment
even though the world has already possessed me
and you, lover and comrade, help my way

with no other choice, I choose my own burdens

**

The ache of poetry is the knowledge of loss;
the loneliness of seeing wonderment
which others take for expected
in a world they don't realize has nearly lost it

Poetry sees the bend in the road leading from

Williamsburg to Jamestown,
meets every soul who has travelled it,
and presses under their weight

Poetry knows that the people of Flathead
live in simultaneous stolen glory
and unaware fortune,
gold rush dreams sure to come
as capital destroys supply,
creating a demand
for life.

Poetry sees her, cruel and cold,
and can't help but see her noble, if broken, fight as well

Poetry knows what once stood in the place
of the bright, sharp buildings of Portland
and Seattle

Too many stones will press a man to death
and poetry is thousands and thousands of stones

We Speak the Same Language to Each Other

It has never occurred to me to write poems
for, but not about, your eyes;
to look through your lens at lines on paper
and pipe buttercream between them.
I'd have to lick my fingers after.
Or maybe you could lick them for me,
wrap your lips--the ones that you press together--
around each of my fingers,
one at a time,
and pull sweet residue from them.
Philosopher as muse.

Subtweeting a Certain Snake

You: dead-in-the-wool
by exceeding stillness,
better satisfied with stopping the train on its tracks
than building new ones,
necessary
to those who would outlast their usefulness.

You slither around half-truths
on behalf of a cause
only part of you believes in;
use up what little remains
of people who believe in it fully.

We are not immune to hierarchy.
Organizational fault-lines making us more
the Family
than the future.
And you, the Fixer.

Must power be played
even amongst ourselves
if we are to rid ourselves of it?

Silver Spindles

Rain in silver spindles
a gradual cascade upon the pavement

the force that carved the Grand Canyon
will one day wash it all away,
even the concrete,
if the wounds are left to heal

you say wool, I say cotton
you say needles, I say diamonds

one time, I was caught in a Virginia thunderstorm
and I didn't need to bathe

even such heavy sorrow as I carried then
was washed by Laurel Run
off the mountain I stood on

Train-Hoppers

You can find the hidden souls of buildings
in every kind of city, or town;
climb over this railroad tracks or that creekbed
and discover the living shells
where people once moved, or plotted, or struggled--
the kinds of stirrings only ordinary people know
when they sense them.
The kinds of stirrings men in clean shoes
and   unwrinkled
shift their feet to, feel on the backs of their necks.

Take the Raleigh Tavern: hordes of clean-cut observers
longed to see the inside, pushed for entry,
while I stood on the street outside caught
by the ground in front of it.
I found out later it was rebuilt for the museum,
and it was outside of it that rousing speeches
of revolution were given.
The Rockefellers painted over the building
while the grimy fury of the excluded
lived on outside of it.
The trees in that town whispered to me
that the ghosts weren't to be found
where they were expected.

And in Kalispell, the rocks and broken bits
of buildings hidden, ugly,
behind the Wendy's and the park
were where you fled as a child
to soul from soulless--
any soul would do.

The souls of train-hoppers and outlaws
preferable, then, to the empty comfort
of suburban plush, of family dinners
and action films, after-school activities
and business classes.

I hiked through wild bamboo
to the old train station on my way
to the bus stop, back then.
I contemplated leaping onto a passing train there,
running forever from the apartment we lived in,
in the pretty new building with the broken closet
I used to hide in.
Two hundred years of Newport News travelers
calling me aboard.
But the train didn't stop there anymore.
Men in clean shoes boarded it up,
men in clean shoes closed the passenger trains,
men in clean shoes made me hide in the closet
and dream of fleeing toward the soul
of what no longer was.

Ode to a White Girl

Oh, but
the sum of her parts--
something amounting to nothing,
if nothing can be called destruction

sweet nothings
meaningless touch
coiled hair weighted by pale skin
and false purity

there are tears,
but does she mourn?

It's not really who she is,
but how--
how she learns from users
how to use

how she learns from the used
how to mimic survival

how anything can be used as a weapon

I've always thought it was funny
how she can pirouette but she can't dance

How Do You Find the Words?

One thing she taught me was how
to be patient with words.
Settle those parts of the body, the
parts that tap and flutter, just
long enough to sink into
the earth, the mud of a moment;
just long enough to listen to the heart beat
in response, not in anticipation.
Take stock of your surroundings.
Tune them out, or pull them in.
Adjust like the focus on a camera,
but take more than a snapshot--
what is it that a moment is
that is more than its reflection?
She taught me to let words slide at their
pace onto my lap; how to wait
on them without a pounding heart;
how to let a feeling pour like cold
water over me, painful and
awakening.
Waiting for words is falling asleep
to waking up; easing and slowing
into brightness.

XXXIV

Your heart, which I sense in the night especially--
whether I can hear your slow breathing
on the pillow next to mine
or must imagine it, miles away--
mutters its passings to me in a language
I know only few understand.

Your sigh is, becomes, my sigh.

How easily I have chosen to stand firmly by your side,
though the standing was like holding my footing in a
  hurricane.
But the river in you grounds me,
guides my path,
even when you cannot understand which way you weave.

At night, at your parents' house,
we made a ritual of wandering through town,
talking of everything we could perceive
under those bright mountain stars.
You knew your path then, without even thinking of it.

You believe that because I am soil; salt; phosphorous;
  potatoes
I am the one who grounds you.

And perhaps, in some way, I hold you to the earth.

But you are the force that pulls, that moves, and I too move
along your path.

Your sigh becomes my sigh.

I have friends, suffragettes, who would tell me never to
  follow a man.
But they are fools, who cut their own trails in the
  wilderness.

I sense your heart, and I see the brightness on your path,
and I guide you along it with me.

"At Least Nothing Happened"

Talk about it without saying it, because it didn't
happen to you--this time
at least not in the places everyone means
but my liver and kidneys still feel hollow,
scraped-out like a melon,
aching with an emptiness only an invasion
can leave
just the way the places everyone means
ached and hollowed each time it really happened.
What is the difference, if still
some *he* took unwilling hold of my body?
At least nothing happened. Nothing that counts.
Nothing exceptional to the way my body,
our bodies, are for use.
Normal wear and tear. Just a paint job.
Just a touch-up. Just chemical fingers
reaching into every cavern of my being,
just I almost stopped breathing, just
no part of me left untouched.

XXXV

She pulls harder than she realizes,
tugging gently at frayed ends and tendrils,
hanging on eardrums,
grasping for the sound of a voice
and the color yellow.

She sweeps up dust;
brushes away lint.

She slides behind,
and ducks underneath.
It's not often someone so secret
is so honest
but her hands are on her hips
and tomorrow matters.

for Tonya

Footing

It was because of the joy you took
in teetering, skirting,
feeling that solid sureness of your feet
when sliding, slipping, uncertain soil
was so near
and the resentment you carried
toward the way my voice cracked
and my fingers twisted around themselves
     please, be careful
—that was why I got used to pretending
I could trust someone else's foot on a ledge,
or a gas pedal.

It was the edge of the highway I walked,
abandoned,
but still I pretended I was just a hiker—
packless, in a skirt and sandals,
a woman alone in the middle of Shenandoah National Park—
to every car that passed by.

A man I knew in town,
eating his grief in white lines
and foaming glasses,
stopped.
He looked me in the eye.
     You don't have to stay with him
      when he's cruel to you
I laughed and told him I was fine.

Edges, lines, brinks, highways—
the difference is when it's your own feet.

Terminology

Waiting for words is the poet's insomnia.
Sink gently, like my bones into the mattress.
Settle my eyelids.
Letting the mind wander is a risk, but
the only way into caverns where lyrics
grow like calcium deposits, clinging
to the roof.

**

We are closing the space for poetry.

We need to-
When we talk about-
The exclusion of-

Terminology is venom;
evolved for protection, but
too often used for offense.

Terminology leaves no room for metaphor,
for *as if*,
for synesthesia.

I propose that poetry is what the commons looks like
in words;
the lyrical form of meadows and forests,
bread and wine.

Do we not realize that enclosures
are what we've been fighting for centuries?

Drop that wine onto my tongue,
spill those sapphires,
pour the act of listening onto the page
and let me free.

Let the now lyric its way into the past,
into the future.

Exposure

Dusk. Tired limbs sprawled like vines,
awkwardly finding places not meant
for organic bodies. A red mark forming
on my forehead where it presses against
the car window, watching cows. The
tin hardness of my mother's Bon Jovi
cassette tape playing from the front, on repeat
for the third time. My baby brother snoring
in his carseat next to me. My little
sisters bickering in the seat in front.
All I can think of is the way our yard
will smell when we get home, the grassy
cleanliness of Oregon soil after a rain.
It has only been a week, but I'm certain
I've spent a century in Idaho's musky desert
weight, the emptiness of hot, dry air and
the eerie, naked feeling that without trees,
the mountains are watching you. I have already
learned to be uncomfortable naked. I
thirst through my skin; humidity as clothing.

Trans Women are Women

It is with corsets, contours,
belts and bustles,
that ever-looming device: *the high-heeled shoe,*
the way of holding one's fingers
more for display than for use

It is to practice how to make intonations;
how to say the words
mattering more than what they mean,
the way the lips are set
when one isn't talking

if there is essence to *woman*
it is only this:
becoming more of oneself
using all the tools of falseness.

if there is difference between *cis woman*
and *trans woman*
it is only this:
whether those tools are seen
as uniform or costume.

Sisters. Deeply sisters. More sisters than
my brother is my brother. You,
I know, understand
how the pageantry is also not
a charade. How being *woman* differs.
Not between, but from. How little
and how much that means.

XXXVI

Our survival is our solidarity.

I hear in her voice a pride
that I know in a way I've never explained

the pride of the Bathtub, of cracking open crabs with bare
  hands, of beasts

the pride of lemonade; of lemons, sugar, water and the
  growl under her voice when she says

trade these broken wings for mine

*you've got to learn to take care of things that are smaller
  and sweeter than you*

the cross my father wears for his nana,
who had hers taken from her in 1915

the place on my breast where mine would lay,
which I tap unconsciously for ground

survival in worlds like ours
is food, water, shelter, breath

truth that pierces, pushes forward, sees

the ocean is rising, so
to survive, we dance

*for Beyoncé
and for the Bathtub**

Gaia, The Day She Swallowed Them All

It was a hot day. The sun was as angry as I was,
licking my surface with his frictioned,
stinging tongue, the burning clean of rubbing alcohol
in a wound. I opened these lips
I'd kept so tightly pursed against the poisons
made of my own flesh, spread my limbs
and stretched these cramped, load-bearing muscles.
I yawned; twitched like a cat waking up from a nap.
I pulled myself apart. In they tumbled,
surrounded by their little beasts, machines, shelters;
seashells versus the force of the ocean. Laughable.
They made noises, small echoes of the scream that
has been in my bones for centuries, leaking
out through mountaintops and the tunnels they dug
into my intestines. Hush, I said. I know. I'm taking you
home.

That Soil Is In My Bones

The draw of cherries. The warm, mahogany
sweetness that I feel running through
my veins, the jeweled prisms of pomegranate
seeds, thick forests, my hair, my blood.
The way cornflower blue eyes
look like the mountains in the spring.
Black and blue irises shouting pain
and beauty so briefly, calling up memories
I didn't know I had. His eyes,
and the lines around them.
The way round toes look in the sun,
the way thick hair makes ropes--this head
is the way to its own escape.

**

I didn't even have to see one.
I named my first book *Iris*, at 13 years old,
because I saw it on a street sign
and something in the pit of my stomach
called for it.
Irises, which grow wild on the Caucasus mountains.
Irises, which come in every color,
opening the mind up to possibility; to words.
Irises: windows.

**

Some of us do fight; see the parallels;
know that if we've been torn
we might as well keep the wound open
and keep the battle going.

Some of us love deeper than we fear.
Some of us think of our enemies
even as we're sent to die.
And every one of us, at the end,
is sorry to those we leave behind,
shocked, afraid.

We all die with fear, but some of
us die with love.

*pour Missak et Melinée Manouchian**

Reading Your Old Diary at Your Parents' House

Overturning your stones, I come upon the must
of dead leaves and moisture and
the cosmopolitan movements of ants and worms;
life making paths through every dark place,
every memory

and what emerges is you-
not radiant, not glimmering, but alive,
the past and the future full in your skin
and your eyes
and the honesty of freckles spelling words upon you
like constellations.

You have been every person I've uncovered
in yearbooks, stories, rocks you've climbed and
people you've loved
and the way versions of you spill through them-

or reflect off of them, something, someone within you
that only remembers itself when they speak its name.

A stack of notebooks, twisting through time.

Mirror

There is something purple about the memories
of human beings you've never known, who died
before you came, but know something about you.
Dark fingers reached to tap my shoulder from after time,
the way moonlight makes skin violet
and voices whisper.
Nadezhda leaned out the window of her
Rue Bonier flat--the one with the curtains
she chose especially for Lenin, a woman's
anxieties becoming fussing
when no one says they matter--
and she told me firmly
that she was looking in a mirror.

To think! I was a liberated woman!
But I had to admit, I knew
from the way it swayed that this ship
was not on a clear path forward.
I knew such seas throw sailors
into unexpected continents,
even with a working compass.

What does it mean to be more
Nadezhda than Lenin; more curtains
than pen; more broken
than misguided?

**

I climb under the bridge;
I want to stand next to the creek, not
above it.
It moves so low, so slowly these days.
I close my eyes and listen to the roundness
of its trickle,
hoping to hear some near-magic mathematical
truth come uncoded in it
like the golden ratio in a sunflower.
Or at least, to be able to pick out the sounds
of the fish jumping out of it
and the moments it splashes over stones.
I hear only a whisper:
you're looking in a mirror.

Upper Middle-Class White People in a Wine Bar

Filmy barricades.
We have to tear them down with our teeth.
Candlelight, tinny strains of music that backstrokes,
poetry and wine
are not, as Audre said, luxuries.
Yet past those flimsy, filthy barricades
are only soulless souls; tired barely-selves;
bodies with limbs seeking just enough honesty
to survive.
A kind of survival I, who have been hungry,
can never understand.
I've never seen anyone enjoy anything
so joylessly.

Memories of Idaho

There is a scent to this place,
dusty brown, concrete patios,
a vague sense that mulch and aging toolsheds
are never too far away
and the way a wide, empty sky
sits heavy on the rooftops.

The uninterrupted sun on my neck
reminds me of the time we carved the Grand Canyon
into the red clay behind the house.
We spent all day digging an eight-foot winding trench
while the sun nibbled on our skin.
It was a useless project; the yard was set to be landscaped
  the next week
and our creation destroyed.
Our grandparents apologized, sorry to us that they were
  spoiling
our artwork.
But we both knew we were mapping out our escape.

You tell me now how, nearly twenty years later, you've
  made it out.
The skin around your eyes becomes small canyons
when you push your words of relief into my hands,
hoping I'll tell you they're true.

**

Memories of nights growing cool and teasing dawn awake
  with playful fingers;
of the way stars twinkle more in the city
and seem to be bigger in the desert;
of the delirium of riding the night out on
whatever high is produced
by a long conversation
and the accidental brush of fingers in the dark--

morning never feels less like morning,
and love never feels more displaced from time.

I felt him before you, under the chatter of stars
in the Idaho desert.
He taught me that love necessitates acceptance
and I opened myself for the first time,
at seventeen years old, to another person.

Ten years later, in the dampness of a Chicago July,
I opened again to you.
Practiced now, but still shy, the stars again guided me
as we walked in circles till dawn, talking through time,
  spotty,
our erratic flight as logical as a bumblebee's odd path
and as imperceptible from the outside.

Today, you and I sit together under the open sky
and the warm sun of a budding desert summer,
our closeness the silence
of love that has become a pattern.

Tonight, we will laugh together under the stars.
Love in time, or out of it.

Her Shoulders

Glass glinting in orange light,
mahogany and brass licking every corner,
wrought-iron wrapping its way around the bottles
and her--
too young for this bar
and too blue for this brown;
a bluebell in a field of poinsettias.

She doesn't like cocktails with bitters
any better than I do,
but she turns down wine
with hunched shoulders--
somewhere, someone presses on them.

And what presses on me
is a drive to uncover; to understand
her blue, and her shoulders.

The Girls in the Stars

Aaliyah Nadezhda and my little bird
sit in the place in the stars
where the conceived of, but not conceived, live.

My uncle Tim holds them on his hips
and points down at his nieces, their mamas.
He tells them one day they'll be born into a better world,
the one their mamas fight for,
one where little girls are born joyously
and the stars follow them down.

They know why they have to wait.
They know how much their mamas long to kiss their eyelids
and teach them how to style their hair.

But Aaliyah Nadezhda and my little bird
will live in a world
where everyone gets to eat pomegranates
and pick flowers
and hold babies on their hips

He's a Democratic Socialist, After All

I fight for the ordinary man, he says,
tripping over his well-ironed slacks and excuses

for such errors as
rolling his eyes

at the thrill and hum and mechanic glory
of *they're just driving in circles*

at the startling genius of the bartender
who can't spell half the drinks she can make

at the honesty behind bus chatter
and crass jokes at a barbecue.

The ordinary man
 -oh, of course, women too-

The ordinary man, as seen on TV
and certainly not as seen on the other side of town.

The Only Good Gemini

My poems have avoided you,
even the lick of heat coming off your fire;
even the breeze in your wake.

My poems have spun themselves around,
cut through parking lots and backyards,
poisoned their own wells
and whispered their words
to avoid you.

Not because you broke my heart,
but because you opened it--
this heart that was battered before it knew
what opening was--
does my pen fear to sing your song,
or of it.

What no one realizes
is that air is not empty
and your wind is a force that can build
or destroy mountains.

Will they see what I see,
or know what I know?

There is still a part of me
that returns to you.
If it were love, I would publish whole books
offering you the knowing of it,
but it is something less,
and it is something more.

You resonate.

And I struggle, and fear,
to put you into words.

for Josh

Like a Drumbeat

They say anything that repeats
is music.

You can taste it,
      lemonade on the tongue,
      lilacs overrun in your garden,
      fried catfish and sweet tea in the summer

      your name in the air--

it's silver, silver, silver
as a constellation,
and just as semiotic.

Sing to me--
I want to hear of thought
and meaning,
beauty and time.

Then sing to my hips
in liquid bestial notes of movement,
and when you feel me the most--
      say my name, say my name.

Turn Around, Bright Eyes

It sure seems sometimes like you can't flip around
and head the other direction until you get all the
way to the far end of the pool. I mean,
it seems like being one step short of the worst
makes it harder to move, like the flipping
point requires being "all of the above," everyone
else just stays where they are. And I
know that's an exaggeration, maybe even a lie,
but how am I supposed to reconcile the
way you're like the shadow of something sheer

Songs of Songs

The way bits of you wrap around me
encircling, sliding,
ribbons of gentle joy in brief memories,
I never feel words alone are enough for you.

Your way needs music, strains that float
landing like a gull on the ocean,
gliding into place on my forehead, my lips,
the place between my shoulder-blades:
tender parts of me, the parts that know you.

Only hold me with your arms.
I don't need your secret places,
only the body you move with,
only your heart against mine.

**

Open the window. I don't want to see you
through glass. I don't want to hear your song
muted by barriers. I want you to look
into my eyes and see your reflection. Open
the window. Open a window. Open a heart.
Open my heart. Open my eyes.

**

Gift for gift, soul for soul,
my words for your butter threads of sound.
Supposedly, a fair trade.
But I've offered you only a nibble

of the feast I've prepared you in secret.
You could gorge yourself on the pages
I've traced patterns of you into,
lovingly, with my own hand.
For a nibble, you offer me a whole helping.

How can I wash myself in your song
when my tell-tale lyrics hide themselves in my throat?

**

How human
that the battle hymn of thumping hearts,
the opera of whispers and a war cry,
lead into the strains of one breast bound
to another; the tension between notes,
the way music sits in the spaces like memories.

I have just short of enough of you.

Write me a song. Sing to me
that embrace, your arms pulling for
a spare moment
saying more than your mouth, or your eyes,
ever do. Let me hear
that feeling, make me sure it is real.
Play me your heart.

Love in a language not spoken
with lips at all. I want to become fluent.
Let me learn you, learn the past,
learn the future.

XXXVII

More than the blood that boils so raw,
so hot in his arteries
and in mine,
and more than the overlapping bits
of programming encoded
in her cells
and in mine,
there is something built into your body, your mind
that I recognize in the mirror.
You, earthen and abraded,
are a more important kind of sister.
Your existence both reflects and layers my own.
You, the same and different,
give reality to the way I see, and know.
You, like me, fight
because we know the same things
and our stomachs, which remember with a mind
of their own, will not let us rest
if we hide.
We are related; we are bodies born
of the same reality; we are healers, lovers in
warriors' uniforms
too accustomed to fighting alone.
We are not alone.
We are two stars, sisters in a galaxy, a galaxy in a
vast, overwhelming universe of souls.
And you and I,
we have our eyes on the stars.

for Yasmeen

Forgive the metaphor, but

you can learn to swallow cheap tequila
like it's a fine rosé,
like you're a girl who deserves fine things
even though, secretly, you're making do
with shreds.
But you're building muscle!

Take in the glint upon the glass,
the way the liquor sparkles under the bar lights,
the clear invitation of the tequila
hinting to you that it could taste like anything.
It could be diamonds in that glass.
It could be joy in your heart.
It could be freedom in your soul.
You just have to swallow it.

Ghosts

Without ghosts,
history becomes cardboard;
flat, dry, flimsy

and cardboard can't make walls,
much less a foundation.

The bricks, and the steel,
and the concrete
have to be built fresh
and this is the hard work of the age

but ghosts can make a building
a home;
a hall a commons;
a factory a place of resistance
and power.

Ghosts can teach us what love means
and how to persevere

and they can teach us how to move
with wounds

의

To forget earth's position in the universe
is like forgetting time.
What is the good of knowing where you are
if you don't know where you came from,
or where you're going?

After sunset, I walk to the park
at the edge of the hill.
Below it, I can see a field of purple flowers
dark against the lowlands they occupy,
and beyond them, the heavy green
of the river.
I know it like my own heart, my fingertips.
I have to force myself to find a bench,
lean back, let the skies wash over me like
a cold rain.

The moon, little sister of my earth,
closer to my knowing, hushes me,
pulls me on. *Look at Venus*, she says.
Big and blue, I can see why she
rules love. I can see the red anger of Mars,
the way the stars arrange themselves
into hieroglyphs, the language Babel reached for.

Is it any wonder the ancients looked
at them and saw gods?

I have to be reminded
that Jupiter will still be there.
My skin is covered with symbols
of the cosmos, my finger-threads to myself

pulling this body from the soil
and into the stars.
This is the curse of *grounded*:
I forget Andromeda and remember onions.

With gratitude to Olly Thorn for reminding me of Jupiter*

To The Men Who Don't Understand

You know we're talking
about a war zone, right?

Not just imagined reflections,
memories folding up from the earth in our path
like a shooting range,
not just a minefield strewn
with relics of horrors past,
but a burning, muddy, thundering battlefield,
alive and dead with danger.

We are talking
about staring in the face of atrocity,
our pasts and our futures filled
with the same threat as the present.

We are talking
about now.

I don't know whether to plead with you
or tell you to fuck yourself.
I only know how much we need you
to understand.
Not allies, but fellow soldiers;
comrades in combat.

The grim, gory awakening
that is solidarity.

Love in the Language of the Liver

Guh seerem kez
words whose tongue feels toddlerish, awkward
but whose meaning reels through me in the way
only words can:
I love you
in the language of my bones, of diaspora,
in the back of the throat
where the body is itself.

Gdesnem kez
it means more that I see you
in g's and k's
than in the sheen and shabby coarseness of English,
stumbling its crass way across our mouths.

We say *jigyars* - my liver - instead
of *my heart* or *my darling*;
we are people of the body, the organs
making their way into our throats,
the meanings of the world never detachable
from flesh.

You, *jigyars* -
mernem djanid

Armenian (Western):

guh seerem kez: I love you
gdesnem kez: I see you
jigyars: my liver
mernem djanid: I want to die on your body (Western
  Armenian saying)

Elegy for Joy*

Once, I watched a candle with two wicks
dance, the bobbing flames pulling together and
apart in unison, a mating ritual soft and
mirroring. Until I realized it was only one
flame, one wick, dancing with its own
reflection in the votive cup. More alone
than either of us thought.

**

Some parts of us know things
before the thinking parts do.

These days, though I carry the memory
of a pear-blossom sun,
I walk with stiff arms and narrow legs.

Before the world was sour,
I walked with the memory of an orgasm
in my hips
and tasted a boy's mouth in my voice
as I sang along with nothing.

**

Some joy is just relief, underneath.
Fingers sliding along the strings of a guitar,

clean air after stuffed synthesizer sounds
and off-key tornado wailing.

Anger from the deepest parts of my lungs,
pre-cancerous, bursting out in the shower
who are you to tell me how/ to keep myself afloat

A hand in my hair, eyes on my breast,
watching the way my breathing changes.

The first tear I shed over him,
rain after a wildfire.

**

I haven't seen a child make a mud-pie
since last millennium.
Do small fingers still find dirt, recognize it,
make use and beauty
of weeds and pebbles, rejoice
over the rare morning-glory or 4-leaf clover,
make jewelry of dandelions,
rim playhouses and forts with Queen Anne's lace
and fallen cherry blossoms?

Do little fingernails crust with mud and sap,
little knees become toughened by scars,
little hands learn to touch small beings carefully,
little hearts quicken at a setting sun
or a coming thunderstorm?

I know the answer. As the oceans rise,
we pull ourselves away from the earth.

Mothers no longer trust her.
And who would better understand her wrath?

**

They used to give factory workers beer on the job
to keep them complacent
but we're born too exhausted now to need
to be sedated.

Who knew that one day we would look upon fury
as a lost joy?

Beer is only a tonic now for the depression
that follows us through our sleepless nights
and concrete barriers.

Our feet so rarely touch the ground these days.

They turn it to poison while we feebly, drunkenly,
resist.

I Implore Us All

Collect. Interweave. Love one another more
than thyself. Grow patience for a
broken humanity;
grow impatient with time.
Learn how to trust with reservation.
Be more of a body, a collection of bodies,
than you have ever imagined yourself.
This is their greatest fear:
that you become more a body than a tool.
That you become an ocean of organic matter,
fighting for flesh and being,
screaming at the top of your lungs: *we are*

See one another
and you won't need them to see you.

Make the way for them to become us.
Make the way for us to become truer
for lack of a them.

Urgency overwhelms need; unravels
an individual life
and stretches us all into wider,
into *we.*

We can't afford to wait until we have nothing
left to lose
to start fighting.

Love in the Time of the End of Times

A shattering. For you, a bombshell.
You wait for the dust to clear. But
for me, the rubble after the explosion
feels like fresh air. Every bit of that
debris was, moments ago, balled up inside
my stomach, imploding on itself like a dying
star.

**

To think of it: *perhaps*
the rosy dawn of *maybe* creeping
its way up from the ground it was buried in.
Love as it invents itself.
My shame uncurls, rolls out like a rug,
stretches cramped legs and reveals:
reveals.
Unfurls my heart and undoes its own being.

**

You open sound, invite my words in,
teach me without instructing.
What will I know?
How will I find myself under, above,
beside you, before and after,
tangled in spirit, in body, in time?
What will we see, what will we hear?

**

I have flung open the curtains,
letting light into corners, illuminating doorways
I never noticed in the dark.
There are so many places I might find you.
Each limb reaching in its own direction;
searching for difference, for sameness,
for the way your hands or your mind might move
in positions I've never noticed.
Would you, might you, guide me
through your passageways
or even beyond?

**

Burning. Ash. The kind of scream
we all know, even though we have never heard it.
I feel comings and losses and--dare I speak it--
deaths
and all I know is what it means to hold close
to one another.
You both, I know, will be with me in the end.
And so these visions press upon me to know
who I will love, in the way only the wall
behind you, or the firestorm before you, can cause.
Love in the time of the end of times.
What it means to cling to humanity.
One more way we must stretch ourselves in preparation.

**

Gentle, now. Firm and easy, while we still can.
Slip into sensings and possibilities carefully,
kindly, slowly but surely. Make way for us,
for all of us.
Ease me apart.
Not in time as it ticks away
but in time as history moves;
uneven, creeping, all at once, everything in its place.
We rearrange like troops on a battlefield;
ready our positions.

Silvery, Violet, Slippery

I've always thought time must have a voice,
or slips around edges and angles
like a squid slithering through impossible holes:
the lie of straight lines
and borders.

Ticking away
as if the way we measure a thing
is how it moves.

Nadezhda, and a lost ancestor,
and the child who would have been
speak to me in the night especially.
Time twists looser around the moon.
Voices reach for me around corners.

Movement, as if it moves the way we plan,
on tracks or flight patterns
and not the erratic maneuvering of a butterfly
or a rabbit.

Movement, with a mind of its own.
Movement, with a voice.

XXXVIII

Whole cities, greenhouses, internet loves
and the grey sterility of concrete
have not freed us from the relief of rain.
We still don't realize how shallowly we'd been breathing
until we inhale that fresh, moving air;
that moisture that coats our breathways
like dew.
Rain is morning. Rain is the autumn.
Rain is a bright moon, high in the sky.

Rain is the moment night becomes cool enough
to lead to crisp sleep.

The stippled sound of drops on the
skylight over my childhood bed
and the way the rain hits the leaves
along Laurel Run in the spring
are orange blossom and azalea.
Somehow, the imposition of wood and glass,
plastic siding, paint in electric colors
becomes landscape in a thunderstorm.
Rain feels almost like forgiveness.

A downpour: transformative justice.

Y'all Snapped for My Ex Even Though He was Taking Advantage of You

Not one of you is a fool
or would be caught dead with him anywhere else

But here is the soul of the Venue:

a broken man entered,
robed in social wealth
and seeking our brown, beautiful love
for capital gain

and, true as rain,
even he was assumed genuine in his vulnerability
and we loved on him
like one of our own

That night, I was the Venue
and not his long-suffering wife

That night, I learned about what love looks like
when it is both honest and unearned
and I learned how sometimes,
you love someone who doesn't deserve it--
not for them, but for everyone else, for yourself

That night I learned what a culture means; a community
What open conversation looks like
What love entails

I learned that sometimes even blind trust is not foolish

for the Venue

I Have Not Left the Place I Must Return To

Songs of return.
Memories becoming flesh
and vegetable,
things lived and known taking on their meaning
in their absence.
To be a prodigal son necessitates a leaving.

What of loves never known; felt and understood
but never handled, encountered,
spoken to and heard from?
What of a soul that can smell the Caucasus
countryside in her inward places
but has never known the land she sprang from?
Can you return to a love you never left, or knew?

I speak for a home
that never raised me.
I speak for a father who shares my eyes
but not the life that caused the lines around them.
My song of return is a song of arriving.
I arrive into meanings
I remember only in my bones.

Patchwork

Their poems have only one thing in common:
the faint strains of a beat somewhere behind
verses that read fresh and modern;
the lyrical flow more to do with rap
than with the hymnal perfumed regimen
of the romantics, of Blake and Wordsworth
and even Shelley (the best of the worst).

Black women pulling out of rap what poetry put there
in the first place;
the poetry of music and filtered tradition
and bits of righteous appropriation,
the lyric of sound-quilts made
of bits and pieces.

I hear in their poems a familiar cadence,
familiar despite being distant,
as familiar and as distant
as the music and poetry of my own people.

The patchwork of survival.

*for Irène Mathieu and Taz Waysweeté in particular; for the
   desperately important history of Black women poets in general*

One Pair Among Many

Finally, the freedom to sink into you,
unmediated, to watch the ways your pores open,
let bits of sunshine out through them,
the way your eyes tell me about the joy
you feel in the palms of your hands and in mine.

Gentle guide, you rest your head on my stomach.
I was built to care for you
and you were built to show me paths
I would never have seen on my own.

Part of a greater whole, we are a kind of complete together.
For three to become three, three pairs must be paired
and to pair with you is a joy I have missed
from outside its place in time.
I have remembered you instantly.
Let me remind you of me.

Dialectics or Teleology or Something

Every seed is a bud
is a flower is a seed--
does every beginning contain its end?

Or are some beginnings an opening like a mouth,
like Pangea tearing herself apart,
like the universe bursting from itself into itself,
into everything?

Is there a closing in those openings, inevitable, a
  replanting,
a collapse and a new bursting?

Hold me now, because I don't know if the closing I fear
is mine, or ours,
or all of ours.

This mouth opens to sing, or to scream,
lips part to receive and to release--
life-giving and bored-into;
given and taken--
to close them is either to guard or to silence.
Or to begin again.

for the philosophers in my life: sorry I make fun of you while I
  steal your shit for my poems

I Can Hear Whispers Spoken in Mud-Song

There are people who understand dirt,
digging, mud and peat,
who are born with it under their fingernails,
feel cold always in their toes,
have dreams of burrowing and burial,
look at their skin and see
to dust you shall return

Those who grind us down under their boots
forget that from soil comes fresh growth.
They forget that potatoes and turnips
can withstand the winter.
They forget the way the earth yawns
and reclaims even tanks and palaces.

I hear voices in my head,
songs and pleadings of the dirt and all its inhabitants,
words from graves and gardens,
rocks and fields
begging to be spoken while I still have my head
above the ground.

**

There is something dishonest about pavement.
Easing the way for what, for whom?

**

I know you, the way of eyelids syrup-heavy
with old sadness,
the way of laughing that comes from the spleen
or the kidneys
and the metaphors you shyly reveal
under cover of a voice made of copper
and mahogany.

We've never spoken, but I have seen in you
potatoes; nutrients from rich soil;
the deep sorrow that follows anyone
who has looked life dead in the eye
and dared to feel their bones.

Music and poetry: as who we are,
true like the green sprouts of an onion,
incomplete like a lifetime only as long as winter.

for Andrew Hozier-Byrne

Rain

Some people settle, nestle like stones in mud,
become old like wood buildings:
the lie of proportion; age relative.
We look at permanence as if it exists.
What about the way some flowers only last a year;
something new taking the soil it once held,
and helped create?
In life and in death, we make the way
for what lives after.

Hegel for Marx, Marx for Lenin,
Lenin for you
and for me,
the way every woman is a reed,
bending under wind and footsteps,
useful and comforting,
flexible and strong.
Underneath.
We only get to choose so much
of our traditions
and we can only remake ourselves
in time.
History can open forward, but not backward.

Years unravel incoherently into more
and more questions.
When? If? How, how?

Theory and poetry are entangled like vines;
like the wild thickness of Amazonian jungles;
like life with life.

You need me as much as I need you.
We need a place if we're to have a commons,
but the commons is not the place.
The commons is the vines,
the flowers--both annual and perennial--
and the light that takes advantage
of every crack, every opening,
everything sheer
to reach wherever it can.
Even at night, the moon supports the sun
in its infiltration.
The moon and the reeds
made way for me,
and I make way for rain.

Self-Activity

Touch me in your gentle earthen ways.
Touch me with the force of the ocean,
hard and moving.
Feel me, soft and between, reaching for both
winter and summer, different
and the same.
There is magic in threes,
magic I have never dared to learn.

**

Am I becoming myself?
I expected to see you both unfold before me,
to learn you, care for you in closer ways,
but I never expected the relief
of a safe corner to work from,
of enough peace to be, and do, who I am
in the face of what is coming.
How much it means to fill only
the spaces I fit into.

Joy, and something I can't name, well up
inside every part of my body,
spill out through my fingers
and my eyes.
This is how I can make you sure:
my body knows better than it ever has,
better than I ever have.

**

In contrast to me, alone, are you free
to be all you are?
And am I free to be only what I am?
We all become more ourselves,
or less what we are not,
by loving one another.

Love in time--just in time--
and outside of it. Love as it belongs,
love as a hint of what could be.
This is praxis. This is human creativity.
This is more than survival.
This is self-activity.

XXXIX

Thundering approach. Battle drums grow louder;
mark their territory in the material world.
Echoes of the future; actualities
tear holes into now with scraping fingers
as we scramble, fumble, rearrange ourselves
into the fight.

Are there others who cluster
and tremble?
Are we one of many molecules,
organizing on a quantum level,
electrons responding without knowing why?
I fear too darkly that we
are the rare moment of foresight
and not the rising wave of bird-calls
in simultaneous alert.

**

You sing sadness more truly
than the man who wrote it.
Simple, human, aching and present,
the hunger and thirst of the body's needs
standing in front of your possibilities.

The currents of that song run through me,
strike me with their way of not being yours,
remind me of you
and the ways I can love you.

The honest truth: love always has a purpose.

**

I release myself into myself.
To you both, I insist upon myself.

I have hidden eyes that can see hearts, earthen angles
on moments,
tears shed honestly from a torn place,
my sacrifice to us all.
My way of being, translated into words,
is my great work.

It is wise to listen
to low voices,
even your own,
buried however deep behind the lies
of history's victors.

Listen to my voice,
because I know things in my stomach,
my skin, parts of my body long ago
hushed, akin to earth
and I have learned to speak in mud-song.

The Poem at the End of the Book

Self-consciously, I consider conclusions.
How to end any book of poetry,
much less one about the future?

Us, we agree not to come to conclusions.
We have to trust each other enough to open,
not close with endings and answers.
There is no we without petals vulnerable
to the sun; without labor pains
and open eyes.

We are not a distraction. This is what all of it means.
I begin to build both a nest and a battalion
out of those who have the same dreams as me;
dreams of war and darkness;
who know in their bones that we have no chance
without the kind of change that breaks
and bends and groans
before it heals.

The end of times: when love has never mattered more.
Tomorrow: one of many toward the hope of a dawn.

References:

1. "Survival translates across…" This poem is dedicated to Anne Michaels, and was inspired by her poetry collection *Poems*. "*Make beauty necessary; make necessity beautiful*" is from her novel *Fugitive Pieces*.

2. "Start Wearing Purple" This poem references the song "Start Wearing Purple by Gogol Bordello.

3. "The Weight of Daytime" This poem references "*La hija de la diaspora,*" which is a lyric in Nitty Scott's "La Diaspora."

4. "Our survival is our solidarity…" This poem references "All Night" by Beyoncé, and the film *Beasts of the Southern Wild*.

5. "That Soil Is In My Bones" The last section of this poem is dedicated to Missak and Melinée Manouchian, who were French-Armenian resistance fighters during the Nazi occupation of France. Missak's final letter is addressed to Melinée and can be found on marxists.org.

6. "♃" This poem gives thanks to Olly Thorn for reminding me of Jupiter, in his YouTube video entitled "Does Philosophy Make You Sad?" on his channel *Philosophy Tube*.

7. "Elegy for Joy" This poem uses the line "who are you to tell me how/ to keep myself afloat" which is from the song "Gun" by Chvrches

ABOUT THE AUTHOR

Samantha Geovjian Clarke is a poet, podcaster and activist from Portland, Oregon. She can be found on the staff at the Unpopular Opinion comedy podcast network, ranting about politics in her apartment until way too late at night, or using "writing poems" as an excuse to hang out at the bar and drink cheap beer. Her podcast *Dirty Pinko Commie,* on politics, poetry, and witchy shit, can be found on iTunes and most other podcasty places. She is on Twitter @comicwisdom and @dirtypinko and if you want to support her work you can become a patron at patreon.com/dirtypinkocommie.

Her first two poetry books, *Tears Shed With Purpose* and *The Knowing of Being Loved*, are available on Amazon.

If you have praise, ideas, questions, or booking requests you can contact Samantha through one of her many social media profiles or at dirtypinkocommie@gmail.com.

If you have complaints, you can contact the complaint department. Of Macy's or something, I don't know. We don't have one.

♥

www.ingramcontent.com/pod-product-compliance
Lightning Source LLC
LaVergne TN
LVHW051353080426
835509LV00020BB/3420